This book belongs to

_____

Presented by

_____

on

_____

HAPPINESS GUARANTEED
In 6 simple steps!

I
WANNA

BE
HAPPY

by

RVM

Sterling Paperbacks

STERLING PAPERBACKS
An imprint of
Sterling Publishers (P) Ltd.
A-59, Okhla Industrial Area, Phase-II,
New Delhi-110020.
Tel: 26387070, 26386209; Fax: 91-11-26383788
E-mail: mail@sterlingpublishers.com
www.sterlingpublishers.com

I Wanna Be Happy
© 2010, RVM
ISBN 978-81-207-5596-3

Printed and Published by Sterling Publishers Pvt. Ltd.,
New Delhi-110020.

PREFACE

Like you, I too wanted to be happy. Everybody wants to, but very few really live their life with joy. Most people don't even know what happiness is, but they are in search of it. I was looking for joy and read book after book; each one giving me a formula that was not very different from the other. But somehow, it was not something practical that I could put into action and would guarantee me happiness. So many authors, so many books, all great books that made me feel good, but left me thirsty for true happiness!

After reading books on happiness by many successful authors and philosophers, I asked myself, "How can I be happy? What is happiness? Is there a way that can guarantee happiness?" I even set out on a retreat, leaving the world behind to introspect with all the possible research material that I could carry with me. My research material included Dalai Lama's *The Art of Happiness*, J. P. Vaswani's *Secrets of Health and Happiness* and several other books, articles, audio books and DVDs. I armed myself with all the possible ammunition on happiness I could find to start my research. And then the 'aha moment' dawned in me and I discovered how to be happy. So I titled my findings as *'I Wanna Be Happy'*.

Who doesn't want to be happy? Everybody wants to, but look around and you will find people in a race to find something that will give them happiness. People are confused between pleasures and everlasting joy. They don't even know what true happiness means, though they feel it and want it. When I found a way to be happy, I realized that I had discovered a simple secret; a formula, which anybody who truly wanted to be happy could use to dance with joy for the rest of their lives. My script is not complicated. In fact, it is so simple, that one might wonder – could such simplicity lead us to such a profound destination called happiness? Yes, it can!

Whether you are someone pursuing happiness or one who is quite content but wanting to be happier, or someone deeply sunk in sorrow and misery, this book will unlock the doors to happiness.

Different people find themselves in different circumstances at different stages of their lives.

- Some just feel they are plain unlucky and can't be happy.

- Some are surrounded by people who just make them miserable.

- Some are suffering from diseases that create pain and makes them feel hopeless.

- Some are so unhappy that they can't even smile.

- Some are overburdened with problems and challenges that they push happiness away.

- Some have just slipped into sorrow after a long episode of joy that disappeared into thin air.

- Some are happy at this point, but fear that they are going to lose their joy.

- Some are happy this moment and unhappy the next moment, and life is usually a yo-yo between joy and sorrow.

And then, there are others who are neither happy nor unhappy, but are still chasing happiness.

Different people are in different states of being and there may be thousands of people who may not fit into the above descriptions. But one thing is for sure – *everybody wants to be happy* and the good news is that it is not difficult to be happy.

I have discovered the magic of happiness and I consider myself to be the happiest man on earth today. You too can be happy, if you program your mind using the *'I Wanna Be Happy'* techniques mentioned in my book. Read this book with sincerity and put the principles described in it into action. Your life then will be transformed and unhappiness will be a thing of the past. Misery and sorrow will not be on your daily agenda, if only you start each day with the commitment *'I wanna be happy!'*

ACKNOWLEDGEMENTS

Writing a book is not easy. I realized that after spending hours, days, weeks and months on my first book – I Wanna Be Happy. And I want to say here that it is not just my effort that has gone into this book. If it was not for the dozens of books I have read on happiness and the numerous talks and inspirational sessions I have attended, this book would not be possible.

I acknowledge with gratitude all those who have inspired me in creating this book.

The editorial team including Pushpa, Anuradha and Sushumna and the design team including Anu, Sona and Sasikala have helped me put this book together. This book would not have been possible without them.

Various friends and well-wishers have given me interesting and stimulating feedback which has been incorporated into this second edition. I am grateful for their valuable input.

Finally, I don't believe that this is my work at all. Inspiration and thoughts come to us from a greater Power. I bow down in surrender to that source of power as I humbly present this book to one and all.

~ RVM

CONTENTS

What is happiness?

*Happiness is an emotion -
a strong feeling that makes us feel good
and brings a smile on our face.*

CHAPTER 1
WHAT IS HAPPINESS?

While the question is very simple, the answer is profound. Though the question is one, the answers are many. This is because happiness is different for different people. But what is Happiness?

Happiness is an emotion, a strong feeling that makes one enjoy and feel good. It is a feeling that makes one's heart dance and eyes twinkle. Happiness creates excitement and builds positive energy. It makes us smile, laugh and creates cheer.

So, while different people may define their happiness in different words, the emotion that is born in all, is the same. It is a strong feeling of joy, pleasure, contentment and fulfillment.

Different things make different people happy.

- A millionaire could be happy making his next million. → fulfillment of desire
- A teacher may find happiness in the examination results of the students. → social relationship
- A singer is joyous when the audience applauds. → appreciation & acknowledgement
- Politicians become happy when they win an election. → desire

Since different things make different people happy, this cannot be generalized. I may find happiness in solitude, while you may find it in the buzzing excitement of a city. And this may change with time. So what makes me happy today may not make me happy tomorrow. So clearly, people become happy with different things and at different points of time in their life.

It is a myth that ONLY money makes people happy. Surely, money gives pleasure, but pleasure need not create everlasting joy. Not all rich people are happy and not all poor people unhappy. Though some people have a few material possessions, they are content and live a life filled with joy and fulfillment. **Happiness does not depend on what you have. It depends on how you feel. You may have everything and yet be unhappy or you may have nothing and be happy.** So what is Happiness then?

I am Happy today – truly Happy! I have shut down my business and live my life doing humanitarian, spiritual and inspirational work. Although I have ended my commercial life chasing millions, I have found true joy and happiness in what I do now. This is due to my current aspirations which give me joy, bliss and contentment. The happiness I derive by doing what I do now is fulfilling. It is everlasting joy! This, I discovered, is true happiness.

Happiness is not just about momentary pleasures. One may be happy eating a chocolate. But that is just momentary. The pleasure soon dies as time flies. True happiness is a feeling that lasts for a long period. If I view a pleasure as a little lake in my life, I would view true happiness as an endless ocean. There could be islands of unhappiness, but these would dissolve in the ocean of joy.

Material pleasures, of course, make us happy, but do they create unending pleasure? They can make us happy for the moment, but they fail to create fulfillment or grant us the peace of mind that takes us to the peak of the happiness mountain. Therefore, what is happiness? It is being able to do things that create joy and bliss which are not temporary. True happiness is living a life of satisfaction, contentment, joy and peace. It brings a sense of fulfillment in whatever one does.

Are you happy? Are you truly content with what you do and how you feel? Do you wake up every morning looking forward to life? Does whatever you do make your eyes twinkle? Does your work make your heart dance? Does the 'feel-good factor' last most of your day, your week, your month, your year and your life or are you struggling through life, not feeling good about what you are doing? Are you dissatisfied with your career? Are you unhappy about life? What is the state of your mind? Are you peaceful with those around you or is your life in turmoil? Reflection on these situations will indicate whether you are in a state of Happiness or Unhappiness.

Though it is possible for others to share their emotion or feeling of happiness with you, understand that only you can feel your own happiness, since it is uniquely personal and exclusively yours. Only you can decide whether you are happy or not. Yes, like any other emotion, the energy that flows out of you visibly indicates how you feel. Besides, it is not very difficult to make out whether somebody is happy or not.

Suppose you see a person smiling, dancing and cheerfully walking by, would you consider such a person to be unhappy? On the contrary, if you see a person with a frown, spiteful, agitated, irritated, angry and upset, would you consider such a person to be happy? So, happiness is a state of mind which reveals itself through one's behaviuor and action.

Are you truly happy? Do you too want to discover the 6 simple steps that will guarantee happiness for the rest of your life?

Remember, it's a choice unlike what most people say, feel or believe. They might say that they are doomed by bad luck or that their life is meant to be full of unhappiness and misery, but

I have discovered that happiness is a choice. Yes, you can choose to be happy all the time, if only you discover the 6 simple steps that will give you everlasting joy.

As you start your happiness journey, you will find pleasures, joy, bliss and fulfillment along the way. Before you encounter them, understand how each will contribute to your being happy.

Pleasures are little spurts of happiness that come from doing little things. You enjoy eating an ice cream, going for a movie or playing a game of golf. These don't last for long. They are temporary, but they make us happy. As long as these pleasures have no side effects, they are fine and must be welcomed in the happiness journey.

Joy is a little deeper and a little stronger. It is something that you aspire, dream of and then it happens. It is a wish that has come true. It is more than just a little pleasure that comes from a little treat. It lasts longer and gives you more happiness than pleasures would. You are waiting for Christmas, preparing for it, then it happens and you are so excited - that is joy. You are planning a cruise and after a month, you are finally sailing – that is joy. While these give you lot of joy, the joy is not perpetual. As time passes, the fragrance of this joy diminishes with other attractions and distractions of life.

Bliss is extreme pleasure and joy. It gives a feeling of "Wow!". It is those pleasures that give you tremendous happiness and those joys that make you dance. Bliss lies on the top of the happiness mountain – the peak. You want to meet your favourite movie star; it is more like a dream. If it is not just meeting, but you get to spend a whole day with your star, your joy is overflowing. You are elated, excited, thrilled beyond your wildest expectation. That is bliss! Bliss also has another side of extreme joy. Bliss comes at the start of fulfillment, doing things that go deep within your heart and soul and pull a cord. Bliss is deeply internalised. The effect of bliss, unless like a pleasure or joy lasts much longer. Bliss can be recalled easily and revisited in a flash of a moment. For example, music can make your heart dance - It gives you pleasure, it gives you joy; but most of all, music makes you blissful. It leads you to tranquillity. It makes you feel intoxicated. To many, meeting their spiritual master gives bliss instantly. The happiness that flows out of a blissful experience is like a river that keeps flowing or a blanket of fog that envelops one. The effect of bliss lasts much longer and the thought of blissful joy is enough to transport one into heavenly happiness.

Fulfillment is the nirvana or moksha or the 'ultimate destination' of Happiness. It is a state of being ever blissful. You don't arrive there as it is not a destination, but you transcend to this peak. The one who has fulfillment understands what the little pleasures are. Such an individual does not feel the lack of pleasure in its absence and enjoys it when it is present, but never focuses on it. Fulfillment is finding pleasure in everything one does and so pleasure exists at all times. Pleasure merges into joy because every experience creates happiness. Fulfillment is a feeling of everlasting and perpetual happiness. There is bliss in all one does because one's thoughts, feelings, actions and attitude are programme to be happy. Fulfillment supersedes the negative emotions that create unhappiness. It focuses on blissful moments that give true joy that lasts on and on. fulfillment is deep contentment in the heart. It is desire that does not lead to disappointment, for it is accompanied by acceptance and surrender. As it suggests, when one is fulfilled, one is full and filled with pleasure, joy and bliss. There is no space for sorrow to enter and one evolves into a state of mystical happiness, cheer, enthusiasm and peace that surpasses the common pleasures on earth.

On the happiness journey, you must encounter all of these and transcend from pleasure to joy, from joy to bliss and from bliss to fulfillment. At first, material possessions will make you happy. But as you climb from peak to peak, you will find joy without prosperity, bliss without possessions and fulfillment emerging from deep within your heart and soul.

Pleasures are little spurts of happiness that come from doing little things.

Joy is a little deeper and a little stronger. Bliss is extreme pleasure and joy.

Fulfillment is the nirvana or moksh of happiness. This is a state of being ever blissful.

CHAPTER 2
THE 6 STEPS TO HAPPINESS

In my quest for happiness, I discovered that anybody could be happy, if only they knew what happiness is and then went about achieving it systematically. Happiness is as simple as making a cup of tea, but even making a cup of tea involves a recipe or a process. If one does not follow the process or steps, it would be impossible to prepare a good cup of tea. Likewise, it is the same with happiness.

Anybody can be happy. You don't have to be the richest person on earth to be happy. For all you know, the richest person on earth may also be the unhappiest that ever lived. Of course, money can give you pleasures, but money cannot directly buy you happiness. While the lack of money can result in not having material possessions which may make us dissatisfied, it is not necessarily true that poverty is guaranteed to make you unhappy. In this materialistic world, it is pragmatic and important to have a decent earning. But, one must be aware that material prosperity is not directly proportionate to happiness. So move on without worrying about how much money you have. Whatever be your material possessions or earnings or wealth, you can still be happy.

As long as you have a deep aspiration to be happy, you can be happy. If you don't want to be happy, then you may have all the money in the world, and yet remain unhappy. So the 1st Step towards happiness is to want it.

Once you wanna be happy, the next step is to know what makes you happy. *If you don't know what will make you happy, how can you ever be happy?* Every happiness seeker must learn this 2nd Step in the journey to happiness. Once you desire happiness and know exactly what will make you happy, then you are progressing in your journey towards happiness and need to move on to the 3rd step.

The 3rd Step is having the courage to do what it takes to be happy. It is not enough to just want happiness and know what will make you happy. If you do not take action, happiness will continue to remain a distant dream.

Halfway through, one must analyze if the process is working and if the goal is half achieved. Surely, there will be some bottlenecks and problems in your journey that will try to hold you back from your dream of being happy. You must confront and defeat them to progress in the path to happiness. Discover this in the 4th Step.

While it is simple for anyone to follow these 4 steps and reach closer to the peak of happiness, there may be a few unfortunate ones who are deep in sorrow as if the quicksand of misery is holding them back from their aspiration of happiness. Well, for them the 5th Step is the most important step that will reveal, how they can escape from the prison of unhappiness and how they can rejuvenate their lives to create new hope for joy. Yes, it is possible, but before attempting the first 4 steps, this group needs to visit the 5th step and then start the journey. The reason I insist on step number 5 is because many of us are entangled in this slot and we need to get out of it. Therefore, it is very important for this step to be a part of the 6 steps of the happiness journey.

People in this step are in a different state of mind. They are deeply buried in sorrow. Their life is surrounded by misery. They wish to be happy, but can they find happiness? Is there hope, even though they seem to be deeply immersed in unhappiness? Yes, anybody can be happy, but they must first learn to bounce back to life. Once they do, they can follow the steps that will guarantee happiness and transform their lives.

And then finally, we arrive at the 6th Step. It is easy to be happy occasionally, but how do you remain happy all the time? This is the magic we discover in the sixth step where each of us can decide how we want our life to be. Happiness need not be a flavor of the month. It is something that can be yours forever.

So far, I have only given you a small glimpse of the journey to happiness; it is not the journey itself. You must read each chapter to understand each step and then put it into action. Once you do, happiness is guaranteed. It cannot escape you, if you sincerely adapt your life to these six steps.

The moment you stop following the process to find happiness, you may sink into sorrow. The choice is yours! If you don't like the fruit you are growing, you must change the seeds that you are showing. And for this, you must have the courage to change. Only then can you be truly happy!

Happiness is the most important thing in life. Almost everything that people do in their lives is done to make them happy. They make money so that material prosperity gives them joy. They work hard to build name and fame so that the popularity keeps them excited and happy. They chase lofty dreams and accomplish achievements so that it gives them a sense of fulfillment and brings them happiness.

If only people knew that there is a shortcut to happiness which they could easily discover, and it comprised of six simple steps that would guarantee joy; then they would escape a complicated life and live simply but happily for the rest of their lives. Happiness is not a distant dream, if only we know what it means and how we can achieve it. Let us start the journey to discover the 6 steps towards everlasting joy, one by one.

6
STEPS TO HAPPINESS

Be Happy Always! It's A Choice
Step 6

Bounce Back With Faith And Hope
Step 5

Beware Of Joy Stealers
Step 4

Pull Your Happiness Triggers!
Step 3

Discover What Makes You Happy
Step 2

Desire To Be Happy
Step 1

CHAPTER 3
THE 1ˢᵗ STEP
DESIRE TO BE HAPPY

Do you truly want to be happy, or are you lost in the turmoil of life, doing things that really don't matter? Have you thought of happiness? There are people who keep doing what they are doing and continue achieving what they are achieving. Happiness is not a priority for them, so it escapes them. But there are some, who stop and ask, "Why am I doing what I am doing? Why is it that I don't have a sense of satisfaction from what I am doing?" And this makes them ponder further. Many of them introspect and then create in them the passion of wanting to be happy. Finding a source of joy and happiness is far more important to them now, than doing what they have been doing. They have started the journey to happiness. They have taken the first step to happiness because they DESIRE to be happy.

Unfortunately, though most people in this world actually want to be happy, they are too caught up in what they are doing, that they forget happiness. Life escapes them and at the fag end of it, they look back and realize that they were never happy! They were just busy accomplishing their goals, and the pleasures that followed one after the other because their achievements, kept them happy for a little while. Finally, they realize that they were just temporary pleasures, which did not lead to happiness.

So, before life escapes you, it is important to stop and analyze what will give you true joy forever. Of course, we all become happy momentarily with little <u>trinkets that life throws at us</u>. But this is not true joy. In fact, these distract us from the true happiness of life.

If you wanna be happy, the first step is to be passionate about wanting happiness and to place it above everything else. Those who are on the journey need to reprioritize their lives by doing what makes them truly happy, by escaping from the maze of life that traps and consumes them. Yes, most of us get so consumed by life that we lose the desire to be happy. We are busy, but what are we busy with? Soon, we realize that it was a big mistake being busy with what did not matter. What should have mattered the most was happiness, and that was never a priority! Those who realize this are most fortunate. They stop and tell themselves, "I wanna be happy." They make changes in their lives. They chart a new course that will bring them joy, bliss and happiness. Those who truly want to be happy must eliminate all the 'ifs' and 'buts' from their lives. They ought to make a decision to be happy today, no matter what. There is no tomorrow. They make a decision to be happy today, anyhow! On their journey to happiness, they burn all the exit routes so that they don't give themselves any options for turning back, only to be consumed by life.

If you wanna be happy, make happiness a priority. More important than anything else is happiness. Keep telling yourself: "I wanna be happy." Put this slogan up everywhere you go and on everything that you see. Everything that you do must have one objective – Happiness. Then, you have surely started the journey towards everlasting joy.

The moment you embark on the happiness journey, there will be many to discourage you or question you on the soundness of your intention and action. To them, happiness as a goal is weird! They are so busy doing so many important things, that happiness is never a priority. While you transform, there will be many roadblocks, chains and magnets that will try to hold you back and stop you. But if you have started the journey in earnest, then there is nothing that can hold you back.

It is time to move on to the next step because you have now become someone who wants to be truly happy. You are obsessed about happiness and passionate about it. Like me, nothing else matters to you too. You just desire to be happy. The second step is to find out what makes you happy.

Tell yourself everyday "I wanna be Happy!"

If you want happiness for an hour, take a nap.

If you want happiness for a day, go for a picnic.

If you want happiness for a month, get married.

If you want happiness for a lifetime, keep helping others.

CHAPTER 4

THE 2nd STEP
DISCOVER WHAT MAKES YOU HAPPY

You have started on the happiness journey, and you have made up your mind that you wanna be happy. Your desire is strong. It's a passion; it's an obsession. You have now moved to the next step – Discover what makes you Happy.

One actually has to delve into the past to find out what really gave one joy so that one may discover what will make one truly happy. While trying to discover what will make you happy, you cannot forget the past, nor can you ignore the present, for things have changed. You must also keep the future in perspective as to where your desires for tomorrow lie. Your list of things that made you happy must first come from the past, and that comes through reflection and introspection. Then, add that list to what currently gives you joy and bliss. Once done, you can get presumptive and start assuming what will give you true joy in the future.

You make the list to differentiate between the small pleasures of life, and those things that give you true joy. Small pleasures will last for a few moments, but there are some joys that are everlasting. When you have an ice cream or a good meal, it will give you pleasure for a few moments. But probably buying a new home will give you true joy that will last much longer. A hobby, a relationship, will fall into a category that will probably give you eternal joy. Some people find joy in music, some in romance, and some in spiritual and humanitarian endeavors. Others find bliss in pets, material possessions, physical relationships and even solitude. You don't have to worry about what makes others happy. Dancing, talking to people, rejoicing in the beauty of nature and shopping are some things that may bring happiness to some. For others, it may just be the job that they love doing. Each of the above might be more specific for you. It could be enjoying a game of Golf, or dancing Salsa, or strolling in the beach or playing with a Golden Retriever. Remember, this is 'your own' happiness list. It does not matter what others feel about this. You have to discover what makes You happy.

So start with the past and write out that list – 'what actually made you happy'. The first step is to make a list.

TABLE 1

	What made you happy in the past? (Use introspection and reflection)	GRADE * H / J / B / F
1		
2		
3		
4		
5		
6		
7		
8		
9		
10		

* H - Happy   J - Joy   B - Bliss   F - Fulfillment

Review all those memories of joy. It was not just material achievements that gave you happiness; it was more often the finer things like emotions and feelings that gave you true happiness in life. Take your time, but list the greatest joys of your past.

Once you have finished, fill out one more table (TABLE 2). 'The greatest joys of the present'. Include whatever gives you extreme joy. It could be anything; your job, your hobbies, your relationships, the people you meet, the way you spend your time, your recreation, your home or your

TABLE 2

	Greatest joys of the present	GRADE *H / J / B / F
1		
2		
3		
4		
5		
6		
7		
8		
9		
10		

* H - Happy   J - Joy   B - Bliss   F - Fulfillment

work place. Analyze every bit of your present, to discover your present joys.

Once through, peep into the future. Put on your imagination hat and visualize those things that in reality will make you happy in the months and years to come. This is not a wish list, but rather a list of those simple things that will truly

TABLE 3

	What will make you happy in the future – IMAGINE!	GRADE *H / J / B / F
1		
2		
3		
4		
5		
6		
7		
8		
9		
10		

* H - Happy   J - Joy   B - Bliss   F - Fulfillment

make you happy based on your past and present and as you would like your future to be.

Now, you have compiled three lists of what makes you happy. The next step is to grade the Tables 1 to 4.

Against each item in the table, choose one of the following:

1. H - if this gives you a lot of Happiness
2. J - if the happiness is extreme Joy
3. B - if the happiness envelops you in a state of Bliss
4. F - if the happiness is everlasting and leads you to Fulfillment

You may be surprised at your grading. Many truths will surface from your past, present and future aspirations. Once you have graded your list, it's time to eliminate and cut down the list to 10 things that will make you the happiest. You have nearly completed the discovery on what makes you happy.

The final step is to try and prioritize these 10 things. Number them from 1 to 10 based on the amount of happiness you derive from each of them. You now have the final list to reflect upon. Look at it and be sure that you have narrowed down and identified your happiness list. If you do not discover what will make you happy, then you can never be happy. You may be passionate, but without focus, your passion will disintegrate. Sure, this list might change gradually as time goes by, but one can modify it. But, doing the list with a three dimensional perspective of the past, present and future will eliminate the risk of a total makeover. This is your happiness list and you need to make a final review before putting your stamp on it. So look at it one last time, word it out perfectly and there you are!

Bingo! You have discovered what makes you happy!

By now, you feel it is your passion that is adding excitement to your happiness journey. So far, you have finished only two steps – you desire to be happy and you have discovered what makes you happy. Now, it's time to move on to the next step.

A word of caution – whatever forms your happiness list, you are going to broadcast it, publicize it and make it known. Therefore, don't put anything in that list which is unethical or unfair or anything that you have to be ashamed about. After all, you must be proud about what makes you happy and if there is something negative, it is time for review and correction, for nothing negative can ever lead you to perpetual joy.

TABLE 4
YOUR MOST VALUABLE TREASURE – THE HAPPINESS LIST

	TOP 10 THINGS THAT MAKE YOU HAPPY (based on past, present and future)	GRADE 1 to 10
1		
2		
3		
4		
5		
6		
7		
8		
9		
10		

CHAPTER 5
THE 3rd STEP
DO IT NOW!
PULL YOUR HAPPINESS TRIGGERS!

Wow! You have your happiness list in your hands. You have the recipe for joy and bliss.

Is it enough to make you happy? Of course not!

It's the 3rd step that is truly going to give you joy. The third step is, 'Do it now. Pull your happiness triggers'. Based on your discovery, you now have a happiness list. Doing these things will surely give you happiness. But, just looking at the list is not enough. You must do it. For instance, music gives me tremendous joy. I know it and I have experienced it, but I have not gone to a concert in months. I haven't taken the time to listen to my favorite music for weeks. How can I be happy? I know that music makes me happy. Now to be happy, I must press the button since music to my ears is sugar to my soul. Music makes my heart dance, so I must pull this trigger of happiness as often as I can.

I call them triggers because it is not enough to load a gun with bullets. To hit the target, you need to pull the trigger. There are many people who truly want to be happy and they know exactly what makes them happy, but unfortunately they do just the opposite. Happiness is a distant dream, an illusion and a destination they always yearn to reach. If only, we pull the happiness triggers and do the things that give us joy, our lives will be transformed. Happiness will no longer be a destination. It will become the journey itself. If we intelligently make our happiness list, we can have joy and bliss everyday in our lives by pulling the happiness triggers with passion. Of course, there will be blockages and problems that may stop us. But we must be committed to doing what makes us happy.

Happiness is a commitment and with half the journey completed, one must keep one's passion and persistence alive. Put your happiness list everywhere. Put it on your laptop, in your mobile phone, in your purse, at your office, in your home and even in your toilet. First you make an effort to create the happiness list. Once done, the happiness list will push you to get into action. These are your personal happiness triggers.

But there are some happiness triggers which are universal. These are common triggers that you may want to add to your list to make you happy. If the triggers you have chosen are unrealistic or secondary, you can reconstruct your list, reviewing the universal happiness triggers. These universal happiness triggers are guaranteed to give you joy, bliss and happiness. After all, happiness is a simple matter and we can control our feelings, by choosing positive emotions that will trigger positive attitude, thoughts and habit. These positive emotions are sure to generate happy feelings. Some of the Universal happiness triggers which follow will surely work for you too and will trigger happiness in your life.

Make Others Happy

Compassion is sure to trigger happiness. When you care for others and take action by making them happy, you are sure to create joy for yourself. Happiness shared is happiness doubled, just like sorrow shared is sorrow halved. When you make others happy, you automatically become happy. It is a natural human tendency and is born from either being generous and magnanimous or from compassion. Dada J. P. Vaswani says, "Happiness has no permanent address, but it always dwells with those who live for others." Yes indeed, the hand that gives the rose, cannot but escape without retaining a little of the fragrance.

Do you want to be happy – then do it now! Pull this happiness trigger. Go and make someone happy and you will be happy immediately. It may be an employee, a friend, a family member or a complete stranger. It's very easy to make someone happy. A smile, a word of appreciation, some kind of help or even a chocolate can make someone happy. That is all that it takes to generate happiness and the moment you do it, you will be happy too. It is a sure way to perpetual bliss and happiness.

Happiness
has no permanent address,
but it always dwells with those
who live for others.

~ Dada J.P. Vaswani

Happiness Trigger 2
React Positively

We must realize that 10% of life is what happens to us and 90% of it depends on our reactions. Often, somebody close to us says something harsh, unfair and unreasonable. Can we control their actions? No, we can't! But we can react Positively! We can choose a Positive attitude. Instead we choose to react negatively and lose the Joy in our life. Our negative emotions don't stop there. We spoil the present moment and pass this on to other people too. We take it with us through the streets and to our work place. Our colleagues, customers and associates feel the negative attitude because we are oozing with negative energy. Later, when we meet friends, we are still negative.

What created this huge amount of negative energy?

Stop and reflect!

A small trigger made us react negatively. If we are positive, we would not react this way. We would be careful and pull a positive trigger, thereby reacting positively.

While we cannot control others' actions, we can surely control our reactions, because they are our reactions. It is a universal law that those who react positively are happy. Those who live with a negative attitude will always attract unpleasantness, misery and sorrow. Imagine living a life with love, hope, faith, confidence, forgiveness and compassion; how can you be unhappy because you are reacting with positive energy all the time? Instead, if you live with anger, hate, worry, cynicism, indifference, fear and jealousy, these negative emotions will trigger enough poison to make your life miserable and keep it that way.

So if you wanna be happy, pull this happiness trigger and don't delay; do it now. React positively. Choose positive emotions. Eliminate the negative energy completely and you are sure to be happy.

Your reactions
are
your choice!
React positively
and be happy.

We cannot direct
the winds,
But, we can adjust
our sails.

We cannot control
other people's actions,
but we can control
our own reactions.

Count Your Blessings

This trigger is guaranteed to make you happy. So do it now; count your blessings. And how does one do this? Just look around and be grateful for all you have as compared to others. It is very easy to count our troubles and most of us do it. We are always making a list of what we don't have rather than counting what we have. I love these words that I read years ago:

> *"I had the blues, because I had no shoes*
> *Until upon the street, I found a man*
> *who had no feet."*

In fact, there is this beautiful hymn, 'Count your blessings'

> Count your blessings
> Name them one by one
> Count your blessings
> See what God has done
>
> When upon life's journey
> you are tempest tossed
> When you are discouraged
> Thinking all is lost
> Count your many blessings
> Name them one by one
> And it will surprise you
> What the Lord has done
>
> Are you ever burdened
> with a load of care

Does the work seem heavy
you are called to bear
Count your many blessings
Every doubt will fly
And you will be singing
As the days go by

Count your blessings
Name them one by one
Count your blessings
See what God has done

Count your blessings
Name them one by one
Count your many blessings
See what God has done

When you count your blessings and are grateful for what you have, you immediately become happy. Of course, there are tough times. Everyone has them. *A problem free life is an illusion and does not exist.* But, just because we have problems, there is no need to be unhappy.

What does this trigger 'count your blessings' do? When you pull this trigger, it changes your focus from criticism to appreciation, from ungratefulness to thankfulness, from cynicism to cheerfulness and from greed to contentment. So do it now. Pull this trigger and start counting your blessings. You have two eyes, two hands and two feet. Many don't have these. Are you grateful for what you have? Do you count your blessings? I always count my blessings and it gives me tremendous happiness, beyond what material pleasures can give and I become overjoyed. So I keep pulling this trigger. Why don't you try it, do it now and you too will find joy.

I had the blues
because I had no shoes,
Until upon the street
I found a man
who had no feet.

Count your Blessings
and Be Happy.

Program Your Thoughts And Actions

This is a happiness trigger that works for many. Try it. It may work for you. Program your thoughts and actions through positive energy power. Many people think that they cannot control their thoughts and therefore their feelings. Sure, we cannot control thoughts, but we can definitely influence them. This can happen, if we program our thoughts, feelings and actions with a power called 'positive energy'. If we keep adding positive emotions to our lives, we are sure to influence our attitudes, thoughts and habits to be positive. Every positive emotion launched into our lives will trigger happiness. For instance, love is sure to trigger bliss, just as hope is guaranteed to build positive energy.

All these positive emotions like optimism, courage, confidence, tranquility, compassion, enthusiasm and humor are positive ammunition that we can program our life with. We can invite these into our lives and by doing so, we will trigger positive feelings that will generate joy and happiness. Sometimes, a great way to program happiness is to just choose happy actions like smiling, joking, dancing or singing. These will pep up the positive energy that is needed to program our life to joy. Do you really want to be happy? Then pull this happiness trigger and you will be surprised to see what is in store for you.

I accept only those
positive thoughts

and

people, who contribute to
my happiness.

Manage Problems Happily

Many people are unhappy because they have problems. I have problems and I am sure you do too. In fact, every living being has problems. The word 'problem' is born from the word 'probolo,' which indicates something that is thrown before us. Thus a problem thrown in front of us is like a challenge. The way we handle it will decide how our life will be. If we manage problems happily, we will not lose our joy while dealing with them. However, if we allow problems to trouble us or agitate and make us react negatively, we have lost our joy and bliss for the moment.

Sometimes a problem cannot be solved. It just has to be managed. Either way, we must learn to pull this trigger and manage problems happily. This means that we must not let the problems manage us; rather we must take charge of the problems. The way I manage problems is that, I accept them with a game playing attitude. I think of it as fun and solve the problem, and remind myself that every problem has to pass. No problem will ever kill me! And finally if it does, well then, so what, either way, life is temporary. So why worry so much about it. I find that with a positive attitude, I am able to deal with problems in a much better way than I would when worrying or being tensed about them. When I worry about a problem, it robs me of the ability to think clearly. It also robs my smile which is the most important treasure I would hate to lose. So now when a problem comes to me, I first smile. Then I welcome the problem as if I was anticipating it and talk to my problem. In this humorous way, I find that half my problems are solved and the other half gets managed without me losing my happiness. Pull this trigger today, not tomorrow.

Use Hope To Cope And Be Happy

I have often pulled this trigger and have learnt from others that this trigger is like a rope. *A rope called hope with which we can cope with all the dope that life throws at us.* A lot of muck that we face makes us feel hopeless as if we have reached the end, *but with hope, the end will turn out to be a bend and our scars will be turned into stars*.

Hope creates joy because it changes our negative feelings to positive ones. It creates optimism from pessimism and it gives us power. The hopeless one thinks that the night is dark, but hope reminds one that it is always the darkest before dawn and soon the sun will rise.

Without hope, we are lost in sorrow. Hope identifies signals that give us joy, like the singing of the birds before the break of dawn. Hope is a positive energy that is guaranteed to give joy and peace. Do you live with hope? If you do, then it must be one of your happiness triggers. If you don't, then pull the rope called hope. Do it now, for this will make you happy forever and ever.

Learn to live with HOPE: Have Only Positive Expectations! This trigger will ensure you live happily every day.

Hope is not pretending that
there is never any sorrow,
It's the knowledge that
our troubles will be overcome tomorrow.
It's the inner strength we call on
to sustain us now and then,
Till our problems lie behind us,
and we are happy once again.

Walk Away From Unhappy Situations

I love this trigger and I have seen many people using this to be happy. At times, we are amongst people who make us unhappy, in the midst of situations that create sorrow and we just remain there. Why do we do that? For instance, we are invited to go with friends for a movie that is sure to break our heart and make us unhappy. We even go to the theatre, but soon realize that the movie is not good. Should we force ourselves to watch it or can we walk out of the theatre? Of course, we can opt for the latter! Of course, we can! Why pour sorrow into our mug of life and be unhappy.

At times, when somebody is watching a TV program that is negative or the family is discussing a negative topic, you don't need to participate in such a negative event. You can gracefully excuse yourself. We must remind ourselves that some situations may not be under our control, but where we are and what we do is in our hands. We can choose to walk away from unhappy situations, but when we don't, we permit happiness to dissolve and be lost. Therefore, we must pull this trigger and move out before it is too late. In my life, I have made it a habit not to accept anything that is negative whether it is people, thoughts or circumstances that rob me of my happiness. I just pull this trigger and it is so easy. I just walk away from unhappy situations. Try it and it will result in you being happy.

If someone is trying to make you unhappy, just say:

"Sorry I cannot be unhappy. My mind is programmed to be happy always!"

To be happy, we must pull this trigger. We must surround ourselves with positive people; people who are full of love, faith, hope, cheer, enthusiasm, energy, forgiveness and understanding. We are sure to pick up positive vibrations from such people, and that will make us happy.

This is quite different from walking away from unhappy people or situations. That will only move us from being negative to neutral but to be happy we need to enter a positive zone.

When I want to be happy, I often meet happy people who are so enthusiastic that I am sure I will end up being happy too. There are some blessed people who vibrate positive energy all the time, and we must try and surround ourselves with such people always. To be happy, pull this trigger consciously.

> **Meet happy people.
> Be with cheerful people.
> And you will be Happy!**

Ignore The Insignificant

This trigger is important for those who worry a lot. They let the small stuff of life affect them and their happiness. They get into every detail and each detail creates pain. After all, life is a journey that we must all enjoy before we depart. When we lose our joy to trivial things, we may find that we win little battles at first, but eventually, we end up losing the big war itself. What is the use of fussing over every small, insignificant issue and losing our peace of mind? Of what use is it to address every tiny, meaningless issue, but in the bargain, lose our peace of mind?

Our colleagues sometimes don't do what they are supposed to do. Sure, they should have done it right. But by getting into the details, we can only reprimand them and in the bargain, lose our happiness. If it is significant, we must correct them. But more often than not, most of the things that grab our attention are truly insignificant and we sweat over small stuff. To realize the importance of this trigger, look back into the past and analyze how much energy you wasted, how much joy you lost while settling the silly issues. In hindsight, was it worth it? Make a commitment to stop now. If it is a habit, start changing it and don't react to insignificant matters ever again. Each time you conquer this temptation, you will be blessed with joy. Finally, very few things in life really matter and the person who understands this is blessed. One must ignore the insignificant and focus on happiness and joy rather than worrying on every silly matter knowing that worry is sure to kill happiness. If you pull this trigger and start ignoring insignificant things, you have started your journey towards joy and bliss.

Happiness Trigger 10
Reverse Your Hurts

All of us get hurt in life. That is life! Friends too hurt us, knowingly and sometimes unknowingly and we feel unhappy. But we must realize that being hurt directly corrodes our joy. So, how do we deal with hurts? Like Dr. Robert Schuller said *"Do not curse your hurts, do not nurse your hurts, do not rehearse your hurts, instead reverse your hurts."* Yes, there is no point in repeatedly cursing the hurt or reminding ourselves of it by nursing and rehearsing it, but the challenge is how you reverse it. The best way to reverse the hurt is neither by expression nor by suppression but rather by forgiveness. When you pull the trigger with forgiveness, your sorrow will turn to joy and your unhappiness to happiness.

Every day, our near and dear ones may do small and big things that create irritation and hurt. The more we rehearse these, the more we are sure of becoming unhappy, because these will create feelings of sorrow. And why choose sorrow if we learn the trigger of reversing our hurts through forgiveness? We are doing ourselves a bigger favour than to the ones we forgive, because we are gifting happiness to ourselves. Of what use is it to repeat and rehearse negative thoughts and feelings? They will grow bigger and bigger and blast unhappiness into our lives. Is it not simpler and more intelligent to just pull this trigger and reverse the hurts? Forgive and be happy. Try it now.

I am going to be happy today,
even though the skies are
cloudy and grey.
No matter what comes my way...
I am going to be happy today.

Use Positive Self-Suggestions

A great way to trigger happiness is to use positive self-suggestions as often as you can. Those who actively do it know the power and benefit of it. Some people wake up every morning with positive self-suggestions like: "Today is going to be a great day." or "I feel great today." or "God walks with me today, so I will be happy." or "I am going to make today a beautiful day."

These self-suggestions act as autosuggestions or automatic triggers that inject positive energy into our thoughts and feelings and it really works! Some people use these autosuggestions as screen savers on their computer screens or as wall paper on their mobile phone. There is no end to creativity here. Some have posters put up in their offices and homes while some put it in their cars and restrooms. Whenever you have the chance of displaying or projecting a self-suggestion, don't miss the opportunity. It works! It will trigger happiness in your life. It's time for you to pull this trigger too.

**Keep repeating
and reaffirming:
'I am happy.'**

Just for today I will be happy.
This assumes that what Abraham Lincoln said
is true, that "most folks are about as happy as
they make up their minds to be."
Happiness is from within;
it is not a matter of externals.
Just for today I will try to live
through this day only,
not to tackle my whole life problem at once.
Just for today I will be unafraid.
Especially I will not be afraid to be happy,
to enjoy what is beautiful, to love, and to believe
that those I love, love me.

Sybil F. Partridge

Many people pull crazy triggers that give them joy. However, it doesn't matter what the trigger is as long as by doing it, you become happy. Some people become truly happy with their pets. Unfortunately, if the pet dies, they don't get another pet for years. They live in a kind of sorrow or rather in the absence of joy, till they finally realize that they need a pet. The moment they get a new pet, their life is filled with happiness. What stopped them all these years? Do you have a pet? Maybe you can pull this trigger to bring you joy but you don't.

Some people truly become happy with kids around them, be it either their own or others' kids. But for some reason, their lifestyle becomes such that there are no kids around. They lose the joy that comes from kids. We are all made in such a way that the child in us never dies. This works for some and doesn't for others, but you could check if this is a trigger that can bring joy in your life. It sure does in mine. Playing with kids gives me tremendous joy.

Another sure way to happiness is to travel. Travel to your favorite destination. It works beautifully for me. Whenever I want to be really happy, I just plan a trip to one of my natural havens – a beach, a mountain or a beautiful lake.

Do you want to be happy? Then maybe, you need to create crazy triggers like pets, travel, kids or something else that is unique to you but is sure to make you happy.

Connect To The Universal Power

Are you a believer? If you are, then you will probably relate to this trigger better. Those who live with faith and believe that there is a power that gave them life can pull this trigger to be happy. It doesn't matter which religion you belong to. But if you believe in God, then you are fortunate to have this trigger available to you. Those who pull this trigger connect with God, the universal power and become happy. When you connect with the spiritual power, you build faith and faith creates Full Assurance In The Heart. Faith leads to peace, joy and tranquility and this builds the happiness in our lives.

There are those who live as atheists. To them, there is no Creator or God, and they are thus unable to pray and find happiness through this trigger. For the sake of being happy at least, it makes sense to connect to the universal power, so as to draw the energy that creates this joy. If you haven't tried it, it's worth a try. The presence of a spiritual connection gives us courage and confidence leading to happiness. It's a trigger you can pull now, whoever you are and where ever you may be. It costs nothing and if it works, it's a big treasure. So why not try it now?

Happiness Trigger 14
Love What You Do
Or Do What You Love

Many people go to a job that makes them miserable. They work eight hours a day, five days a week and hate what they do. How can they be happy? To them, there is a simple prescription to joy. Love your job or Leave your job. For if you don't love your job, not only will you be unhappy, you will never be successful. Then why drag through something in life that has no meaning. Why not rather do what you love and be Happy?

There are so many opportunities today that you can craft out and do whatever excites you and makes you happy. You don't have to do *something*; you can choose to do what you like. If you choose a job that excites you, it is no more a job and thus it will make you happy and give you joy. So don't continue doing something you hate. Quit. Do it now. You would be doing your employer a favour too!

But what if you are in a situation where you can't do what you want to do. Then the least you can do is try to enjoy what you are doing. Yes, if you can't do what you love, then try to love what you do. If you do, you would be happy and this is the most important factor. Whatever be the case, learn this trigger and implement it. Never do what you don't love, because you can never be happy. If you have no choice, then start enjoying what you are doing. Find a way to make your work exciting. Make it fun and not only will you get it done, but you will also get to enjoy life much more and be happy.

Love your job
or
Leave your job!

Stop And Change

Many people just keep on doing what they are doing and they complain and whine about their happiness. It is strange but true. If you don't like whatever you are doing, why not stop and change. You may be in a relationship that is making you miserable. Why continue? Why not stop and change? Whatever is giving you unhappiness is not compulsory most of the time. You can make changes, but you must have the courage to stop. So stop now and pull this trigger. Stop and change whatever is causing you misery. Find out what it is that will create joy. Trigger happiness in your life. If there is a relationship you must get into, do it now. If there is a relationship you have to end, end it now. If there are friends who are making you unhappy, you must stop and talk to them and not continue to live miserably. It may just be a situation at home or office that is troubling you so stop and change that.

Each of us might have different things that hold us back from happiness that we need to stop and change. I know a person who was in a bad relationship for years. Every day he would complain and cry about the relationship he was in. But he continued till one fine day he decided this must stop. He confronted the situation and it changed forever. Very often, relationships can give us tremendous happiness or unhappiness. It is very important that we evaluate our relationships and ensure we are in positive ones. Review this trigger. Is there something that you must stop and change to give you happiness?

If there is, then do it now.

Many of us forget to live
and enjoy the present moment.
Instead of enjoying what we do or can have,
we dream of things beyond our reach
and become unhappy.

Refuse To Be Unhappy

How can someone make you unhappy without your permission? After all, being happy or unhappy is a feeling or a behavior that is born out of our reactions. We cannot control people's actions, but we can control our reactions. People may try to hurt us, but we can refuse to be unhappy, because unhappiness is a choice that comes from our reaction. Do you wanna be happy? Then this is an important trigger you must pull all the time – refuse to be unhappy. Whatever be the circumstance in life, we can choose to be happy and refuse to be unhappy. Do you pull this trigger in life or do you find yourself unhappy against your wishes? Whenever you feel unhappy again due to others actions, stop and tell yourself, "I refuse to be unhappy" and change your reaction from that of unhappiness to happiness..

To be happy,
refuse to react
unhappily.
Be Happy
instead!

Are you hurt?

**To be happy,
don't curse your hurts,
don't nurse your hurts,
don't rehearse your hurts.
Just reverse your hurts.**

Smile

Have you tried this trigger? It is magical and it works wonders, both for yourself and for the one who receives your smile. It's ironical that though it costs nothing, people do not want to smile. What happens when you smile at somebody? They smile in return and both you and that person become happy. Although it is such a simple and effective trigger, it is not used in most situations in life. However, since you have decided that you want to be happy, it is a great trigger to adopt. Keep this trigger loaded and ready always. When you meet the next person, just smile and see how much warmth it radiates. Not only will it make you happy, it will make others happy too and this in turn will give you joy. While there are some people who are always smiling, some others have not learned this art at all.

When you make smiling a habit, you are encompassed with happiness since you emit happy vibes to others as well as receive happy vibes in return. Have you made smiling a habit? If not, pull this trigger and start today. Smile and you will see and enjoy the magic it brings. Challenge yourself to smile all the time and you will find yourself happy always.

Essential Daily Triggers

Apart from these triggers, there are essential triggers that we cannot ignore. If we don't pull these triggers, we may end up in a soup of unhappiness.

Taking care of our health is one such trigger. If we are careless and do not take care of our health, we may end up in pain and suffering which will create sorrow. Therefore, as an essential daily trigger, we must take care of our bodies and if we have a problem, we must go to a doctor. Ignoring a rotten tooth for example, may lead to a complicated root canal surgery that will surely give us pain and unhappiness.

Sometimes, just food can affect our happiness. Certain type of food makes us happy, but certain others pull us down and make us uncomfortable and unhappy. We must identify what kind of food nourishes us and what can rob our smiles away. If we are committed to happiness, we must learn to monitor and control our diet so that we are happy all the time.

Another essential daily trigger is the type of thoughts we think. Sometimes negative thoughts enter our mind and create unhappiness. If we are conscious about joy, we can fix a filter and stop these thoughts from sinking into us. As they appear, we can re-direct them away, so that they don't enter our domain to make us feel unhappy.

There are many essential daily triggers that together form a trigger.

Another one is peace. Many things rob our peace of mind and lead us to unhappiness. Once we become conscious of what robs us of our peace of mind, we will proactively choose those things that give us peace. There are many more that can be added to this list. Essentially in our daily lives, we must proactively accept and do whatever leads us to happiness.

Be generous in pulling the universal happiness triggers as well as those of your own.

You now have a list of happiness triggers that are universal as well as those from your own happiness list. Pulling these triggers is a sure way of bringing joy in your life. But just like the trigger of a gun that needs to be pulled to release the bullets, these triggers too must be pulled into action. Surely, your happiness list has assured triggers and some of these universal triggers will work for you. Together, they are guaranteed to make you happy.

The next time you are feeling down and miserable, stop and pull these happiness triggers and you will see happiness coming in and transforming your present condition. Be lavish in using these triggers, for the more you pull happiness triggers, the more you will experience joy and happiness.

CHAPTER 6
THE 4th STEP
BEWARE OF JOY STEALERS

Beware! You have just climbed three important steps on the ladder to joy and happiness. You not only have a strong burning desire, but have also discovered what will make you happy. You want to pull the happiness triggers that will trigger your happiness. But now, it's time to be careful. Commonly, we have read signs that say, 'Beware of dogs' everywhere we go. Fortunately, dogs rarely harm us. There are poisons which are more harmful that you must beware of. I call them "Joy Stealers". They are the thieves that rob us of our most valued possessions – joy and happiness. They are strong negative emotions that poison our minds and devastate us. Some of them are anger, jealousy, fear, guilt, temptation, worry, revenge, hate and doubt. These poisons enter our lives and without our slightest knowledge, walk away with our bliss. You must beware of all the joy stealers. This is because we work hard to build a passion for happiness and then persistently discover what makes us happy and powerfully pull each trigger to create happiness. But, the poison of negative energy can nullify all our positive efforts when it enters our lives. And therefore, we must remember, Step 4 - Beware of Joy Stealers. We must keep them away. We must consciously eliminate these negative emotions from our thoughts and attitude. Whenever they appear, we must shoot them down ruthlessly. Let us analyze a few of the joy stealers.

1. ANGER: Anger is a dangerous terrorist that starts as a spark, but burns out our entire emotional strength. You may

be the happiest person on earth, but the moment anger enters your life, it flares up and brings out the worst in you. You lose control and explode, not knowing what you speak. The force of anger is such that it can create irreparable damage. It is a strong negative poison that erupts because of various reasons. However, it is a reaction and can be controlled. If we do not burn anger, it will burn us and destroy our joy and peace. Normally, when this joy stealer enters our lives, we try to suppress it, but it will surface again. Sometimes we try to express it. But it doesn't end there; it only flares up worse than before. The only way to conquer anger is through forgiveness which is a positive emotion that can nullify anger. Beware of this joy stealer. Take charge of it before it consumes you, and if it ever does, be ready to forgive and forget so that the anger subsides and happiness is restored.

2. JEALOUSY: Jealousy is another fire that can burn us. We may be living a life of joy and bliss but suddenly and foolishly, we lose our happiness because we become jealous of others. Jealousy is thus a joy stealer. The moment it enters our lives, it walks with our bliss. It is a strong negative poison that can steal our joy. I had a friend who was very happy because he bought a new Mercedes Benz. We went for a test drive and he was excited and full of joy with his new car. Suddenly his neighbor passed us by in his new BMW. My friend became upset because he was jealous of his neighbor's BMW and all his joy disappeared. Jealousy stole his happiness. Just think about it. Should we let such a joy stealer take away our joy? We must beware of jealousy and when this ugly poison surfaces, we must talk ourselves into being content with what we have. We must learn to be grateful and satisfied. Peace will be restored if we are intelligent enough to let jealousy pass by, rather than give it place in our hearts. If we do, it will enter forcefully and rob us of all our happiness.

Happiness does not come when we have more of something. In fact, greed steals our happiness

3. FEAR: Fear is dangerous, for it can paralyze. The acronym for FEAR is 'False Expectations Appearing Real.' Yes, fears may be false, but this joy stealer is an expert in exaggerating dangers and building strong negative emotions that will steal our happiness. Beware of fear; for once it enters our lives, our peace of mind exits. We must learn to live our lives with courage and confidence – the positive emotions that can conquer fear. When fear appears, we must consciously attack it and make it disappear.

4. GUILT: All of us, sometime or the other, experience the emotion called guilt in life. When we do something wrong, we feel guilty and this guilt steals our happiness. But why should we feel guilty? Nobody is perfect and when we err as human beings, we must make amends. Therefore, instead of letting guilt corrode our soul, we must proactively and positively accept our mistakes and try to make good in place of the wrong done. This way, we remain positive. On the contrary, if we live with guilt, we harbor a strong negative poison that will make us unhappy. This joy stealer can walk away with all our joy and bliss. Therefore when, guilt appears, we must be honest and sincere, and with humility accept our wrong doings. We have to try our best to do good, thus eliminating the negative poison. Never feel guilty. Learn to deal with guilt if ever it shows up again.

5. TEMPTATION: Many of us get tempted to do something ethically wrong. Sometimes, we do these actions to be happy, not realizing that we can never be happy with unethical actions. Some young children steal something that they would like to have, but when they realize that their temptation led them to robbing, they feel miserable. We must hold back from temptation or any negative emotion that will create unethical happiness. Even though we may have temporary joy, this will emit lot of negative fumes which will suffocate our happiness.

The short term joy is so insignificant when compared to the long time misery that temptation creates. Therefore, we must not give into temptations, as they are joy stealers dressed up as happiness triggers. They trigger unhappiness and not joy in the long run.

How do we deal with temptation? We must learn to evaluate and differentiate temptation from the true happiness triggers and choose to pull those triggers that will genuinely make us happy and stay away from temptation.

6. WORRY: It is a negative poison and a primary joy stealer because it eliminates the ability to think with reason and brings along with it fear. When worry occupies our minds, it starts consuming our happiness. It can be viewed as a monster that feeds on joy and bliss. We may be perfectly normal, happy people, but when worry occupies us, it starts eating our peace of mind and troubles us like a parasite robbing us of all joy. Just like any other negative poison, its vicious fumes occupy our peaceful and tranquil minds, making them unstable. Since it comes along with fear, it threatens and destabilizes our very being. For those who have experienced worry, it is not difficult to comprehend the damage that it causes. When worry enters, we must not give it place. We must confront it with positive emotions like faith, courage, calmness and tranquility. If it is blocked from entering, we can be happy, but once it enters, it destroys. Therefore, we must be wary of it.

7. REVENGE: Revenge is another joy stealer. It is so powerful that it can create more momentum than any positive emotion. Normally when somebody harms or hurts us, our natural reaction is to set the score even. We are not used to forgiving and so, we let the negative emotion called revenge take charge of our hearts and minds. At that point of

time, we don't realize it. While it is natural to want revenge, it will steal our joy. Besides, whatever we may get by revenge will be far more inconsequential compared to the damage that revenge causes. Think about it; when somebody harms us, we create negative poison within us that robs our peace and tranquility. Then, we act negatively to make good and temporarily get some satisfaction out of revenge. But is that true joy? On the contrary, once revenge is taken, we feel even more miserable having behaved with such negative poison. The right approach is to beware of revenge and not let it build a foundation in our hearts. Let us eliminate this joy stealer, for it may come in pretending to bring us satisfaction, but leaves with all the joy and happiness that once belonged to us.

8. HATE: It is another deadly poison, for it burns up our heart – a place where love is born, and from where joy and happiness vibrates. It is most unfortunate that some people are overcome by hate, because with hate in command, they are incapable of being happy. Therefore we must be very careful of this joy stealer and not let even signs of it get close to us. By principle, I don't hate anybody even if I dislike them; I nullify that feeling rather than letting it grow into hate, knowing that if hate appears, then happiness will disappear. Those who live with hate in any form are incapable of being truly happy. Such is the power of this negative poison. Therefore, beware of hate and the only thing you should hate is hate itself.

9. DOUBT: Doubt is the opposite of faith. The moment you doubt, you have no faith and therefore this negative emotion can be devastating. It is a trickster that comes to play mischief into a normally positive, happy mind. Doubt is negative and it can never have a positive consequence. In

fact, like the other joy stealers, its goal is to rob us of our happiness. Therefore, we must be wary of doubt and confront it with faith, when it appears in order to eliminate it. The moment we allow doubt to enter our lives, it starts its tricks by eating up faith and confidence, and slowly steals our peace and bliss. It must be encountered and eliminated, for in doing so we will be peaceful and happy.

These are some of the joy stealers that can steal our happiness.

There may be many more. But whatever be the joy stealer, we must not make space for these negative poisons in our life. We must ruthlessly and unconditionally eliminate them so that they are completely distanced and eliminated from our life.

We protect ourselves from the burning sun, from pouring rain and from dangerous waters by using lotions, umbrellas and life guards. But, we don't protect ourselves from the dangers of unhappiness. Imagine you are walking in a park and come across a dangerous insect. What would you do instinctively? You would either try to kill it, hit it or move away. Yet when it comes to unhappiness, we don't take the same approach!

We must be wary of these negative poisons knowing that our first 3 steps may be destroyed in a moment if we do not adopt the 4th step to happiness. While we are busy pulling happiness triggers, let us not ignore the joy stealers and protect ourselves from them. Both are equally important in creating the bliss that we seek.

How can I be happy?

I am sinking in sorrow.
You can,
if you learn to bounce back.

CHAPTER 7
THE 5th STEP
BOUNCE BACK WITH FAITH AND HOPE

While writing about the happiness journey and formulating steps that guarantee happiness, it becomes essential to cover a possible situation, where one's life has been captured by unhappiness and sorrow. Is there still hope? Can such people still turn around and be happy?

People in deep sorrow, often sneer at the thought that they can always be happy. To them happiness is a thing of the past, it's gone forever never to return. They regret and rehearse. They think and curse. They have lost the hope of being happy ever again.

To them, this is the recommended trigger to happiness. They have to bounce back; they have to SNAP OUT of sorrow. They have to escape from misery. They have to eliminate unhappiness and this happens when they decide to bounce back with FAITH and HOPE. They will then cope with the tragedy of life and reverse it.

The two key pillars to help one bounce back are: faith and hope. Without these two, you cannot escape from sorrow that has taken charge of your life. It has virtually strangled you emotionally; it has paralyzed and ruined you. But you can still bounce back. The negative influence in such a situation is very strong and one has to snap out of it with the faith that they can be happy again and with the hope that they can eliminate sorrow altogether. Once these two pillars are strongly laid, then the seeker of happiness can start the journey by desiring to be happy.

A normal aspirant can desire happiness even without faith and hope, as there are no negative influences. But for one who is imprisoned by sorrow, there is a necessity for faith and hope to help them bounce back. The aspirant must not just desire to be happy, but discover what made them happy. Happiness can be restored by pulling the happiness triggers and making an effort not to permit any more joy stealers to enter. The problem that this aspirant will face is this: since sorrow has taken charge, every effort to be happy will be encountered by a resistance with negative energy. Thus, one has to take the same steps (1, 2, 3 and 4), but with an extra dose of faith and hope that will help them bounce back. Faith will build a foundation that will eliminate fear and doubt. Hope will create positive expectations that make way for joy. These two will form the two pillars on which happiness can be rebuilt.

Many people are in such a state of unhappiness in their lives, that they are not able to start the happiness journey. Then there are others, who even though they have started the happiness journey, are unable to proceed as sorrow has captured them back. To all such aspirants, happiness is just one more step away. They need to bounce back from unhappiness by believing that they can be happy again and hoping that their lives can once again be full of bliss. With this belief and hope, create a desire for happiness.

Discover your happiness list and then do it; and pull the happiness triggers. Don't let anymore sorrow enter. Beware of joy stealers and with the positive energy that you are armed with, eliminate the negative poison. You will slowly start feeling the bliss and the joy from this journey. If you are committed and passionate, nothing can stop you. With faith and hope, you will be able to bounce back.

Faith and hope -

will help you Bounce Back!
They are the 2 magical pillars
that will prevent unhappiness
from taking charge of your life.

CHAPTER 8
THE FINAL STEP
BE HAPPY ALWAYS! IT'S A CHOICE

Be Happy Always! It's a choice. You have reached the last step of the happiness journey. The challenge now is to be happy always. You have been enjoying the positive vibrations that came from pulling the happiness triggers. You have a clear map. You are passionate and truly desire to be happy. You know what is going to make you happy and you know what you must do. You are also aware of the joy stealers. You are all set. You must now choose to be happy. The challenge however, is to be happy always. It is not enough to have intermittent spells of happiness. Happiness must be continuous and in abundance and this is possible if you have clearly understood the 6 steps.

Remember, happiness does not depend on material possessions. You may not have everything, but you can still be happy if you know how to pull the happiness triggers as well as know what gives you happiness. Doing so, you are moving one step closer in the journey of joy.

The key to being happy always is to fill your life with positive energy that will trigger happiness in your life. If you make positive energy a part of your daily lifestyle, you will build a positive attitude, and a life full of positive thoughts, feelings, actions and habits.These will trigger joy into your life and you can be happy always. But, if you are not careful and let negative emotions take charge, then your journey may be attacked by sorrow and unhappiness. Unless you bounce back, you will sink into misery. The choice is yours. Nothing in this world is

Happiness is a choice.
You may have everything and yet be unhappy.

You may have nothing and still be happy!
You need to choose to be happy!

more important than being happy. It is our most valued possession that has no price tag. All the money in the world cannot be exchanged for joy and one must value one's moments of happiness. One must treasure happiness and work hard towards being happy always. After all, it is a choice and happiness cannot escape one who is passionate and persistent in its pursuit.

Don't forget the steps to happiness and remember that **happiness is the journey** and not the destination. Keep your list of happy priorities handy and whenever you feel low, pull one of those triggers and raise your happiness levels. Don't delay pulling any of the universal triggers that can give you joy instantly and beware of any joy stealers that may come, and eliminate them immediately. Happiness can't escape you. It can be yours forever, provided you follow the steps.

Mr. Cheer

Before we end, I would like to share the story of Mr. Cheer. To maintain anonymity, his name has been changed, but I cannot forget the impact he had on me by being cheerful and happy at all times. It may not be wrong to say that I was largely inspired by him to be happy always.

Mr. Cheer was not at all wealthy, but he was the happiest man I knew. He was always cheerful and smiling. Every day, he would go around serving suffering humanity in various orphanages, destitute homes, hospitals and hospices. He visited the poorest of the poor to bring a smile on their face, giving them a packet of biscuit, a fruit or a meal. With his own warm hands, he served them with a radiant smile. He would say, "Be cheerful." to everyone that he met.

Mr. Cheer did not have expensive cars or possessions, nor did he own much property or have material wealth. But he was the richest in joy and happiness. His life is a testimony that one can be happy without money and material wealth. Mr. Cheer had a clear purpose – to serve the poor and make them happy. To those he served, he was like a Santa Claus, but one that came every week without fail giving away goodies. Such was his life. He did this for many years. One day, he was diagnosed with cancer. His schedule did not change and he continued to visit the charitable homes and institutions, but his condition deteriorated. His suffering increased and as time passed he became bedridden. All through his illness, for as long as he could, he continued his visits with a smile and his trademark cheer.

I went to visit him when his disease seemed to be defeating him. Even in his deepest and most painful state, he was cheerful. He had no regret, no complaints, not even questions as to why he had to suffer with cancer. He still greeted me cheerfully and although, he was in his deathbed, he was cheerful. His attitude made my heart stop for a moment, as it made a deep impact on my life. I knew him for decades, but no words can express the respect I had for him for living his philosophy of being cheerful at all times and making others happy.

A few weeks later, he died, leaving behind a vacuum of emptiness in all those whom he touched. No more would they be able to see this happy old man on his weekly rounds.

Mr. Cheer made a tremendous impact on me. He taught me that you don't have to be rich to be happy. He showed me that

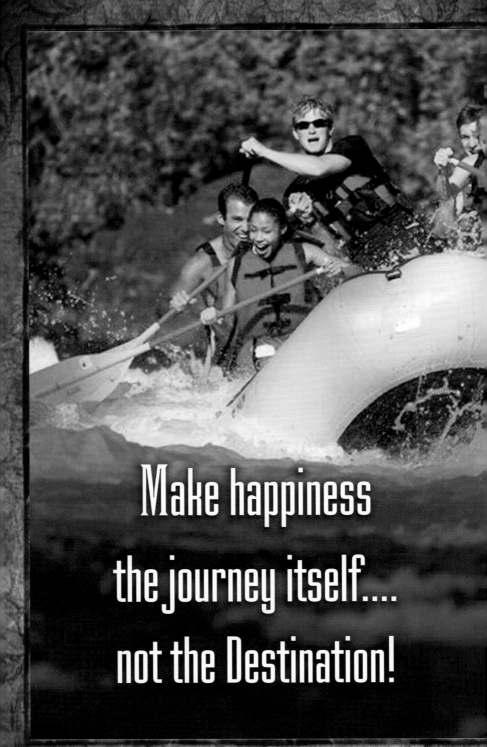

Make happiness
the journey itself....
not the Destination!

if we do what is dear to our heart, we could be joyous. He also revealed his secret: that making others happy was the simplest secret to bliss and fulfillment. I recall what a glow he had on his face! Though his needs were simple and he lived a simple but happy life, he had amassed a great treasure of cheerfulness, enthusiasm, joy and bliss. He carried a begging bowl for anyone to donate to the suffering humanity he cared for. He was not shy to do this, for it gave him joy.

What an inspiration Mr. Cheer has been!

People like Mr. Cheer who live exemplary lives made me realize what true joy is. I have myself experienced this fulfillment and know that it does not come from gold and diamonds, cheque books and property, airplanes and motor cars. Yes, all these pleasures are great, but at the end of the day when the head hits the pillow, if you are not truly happy, all these have little meaning.

Thus at the age of 40, I stepped out of an active materialistic world. I realized that life was more than just making millions, more than adding zeros to the wealth we possessed, more than building a bank full of assets and material possessions. I stopped all that and decided to spend my life doing what made me happy – humanitarian, spiritual and inspirational work. I transformed and rejuvenated my life and the last few years have given me more joy than all the decades that preceded them.

The joy that comes from giving, the love from inspiring others and the satisfaction from serving and sharing is priceless.

Sometimes, I am viewed as a maverick, but it has not changed my decision to transcend from a world of wealth to a life of bliss. Rather than creating pleasure from the things money can buy, I now, enjoy fulfillment from things that money can't buy. While I do agree that money is important to live well, to make a meaningful difference, I have concluded that money is not everything. Happiness is a choice. It is a state of mind and anyone can be happy if only they discover its true meaning and then walk towards it.

The greatest challenge is not choosing to be happy now, but choosing to be happy always. The best thing to do is to keep this book beside you at all times, to remind yourself that you wanna be happy always. Happiness is guaranteed if you pull happiness triggers and stay away from joy stealers. If you make up your mind to be happy, no one can steal the joy from your heart and the smile from your face.

God, grant me the serenity
to accept the things I cannot
change, the courage to change the
things I can, and the wisdom to
know the difference!

Learn the art of
being happy always!

Summary

You don't have to be a millionaire to be happy. Anybody can be happy!

You too can be happy now and always.

HAPPINESS IS A CHOICE.
We can *choose* to be happy or unhappy.

Some people have everything yet they are unhappy, whereas some have nothing yet they are happy.

HAPPINESS is an emotion, a strong feeling that makes one enjoy and feel good. It is a feeling that makes one's heart dance and eyes twinkle. Happiness creates excitement and builds positive energy. It makes us smile, laugh and creates cheer.

Happiness is a journey,
not a destination.

The journey consists of 6 steps.

First step — wanting to be happy.

Second step — knowing what makes one happy.

Third step — doing what gives one happiness.

Fourth step — staying away from misery.

Fifth step — being able to bounce back with faith and hope.

Final step — being able to choose happiness always

It is that simple!

THE 1ST STEP: DESIRE TO BE HAPPY

Unless you are passionate about being happy and living joyously, how can you ever be happy? The first step is that you must have a burning desire and a strong aspiration to be happy. Once you have that, you will have started on the happiness journey.

THE 2ND STEP
DISCOVER WHAT MAKES YOU HAPPY

How can you be happy, if you don't know what makes you happy? So introspect and find out what made you happy in the past. Analyze what is making you happy today and imagine what will make you happy tomorrow. Will this create your magical happy list? Do you have your happy list ready now? If yes, go on to the next step.

THE 3RD STEP
DO IT NOW! DO IT, TAKE ACTION!!!

You already know what makes you happy. Now, it's time to pull the happiness triggers. Happiness is just an intention away and will be yours with action. Let nothing stop you from pulling the happiness triggers. Be happy and move to the next step.

THE 4TH STEP: BEWARE

You are busy pulling happiness triggers. It's great you are happy! But wait just a minute, beware of joy stealers. These thieves silently enter into your life and make you unhappy. Beware of the joy stealers like anger, hate, worry, revenge, jealousy and temptation. Don't let them in because if you do, happiness will go out.

THE 5TH STEP: BOUNCE BACK

At times, you are deep in sorrow and cannot pull the happiness triggers as you are stuck in misery and sunk in despair. Is there a way out? Yes, you must learn to bounce back. Take help of the two pillars – Faith and Hope. You can then bounce back, rejuvenate and live a transformed life of joy.

THE FINAL STEP

Be happy always. Happiness is not momentary. It is a way of life and if you wanna be happy always, you must learn to choose happiness in all that you do. By pulling happiness triggers and staying away from joy stealers, it is possible to be happy all the time. Start now; live with joy and bliss today and every day.

MY HAPPINESS COMMITMENT

Today, I promise that I shall be Happy all the time. I am making a personal commitment and vow that I shall not let JOY STEALERS like anger, jealousy, greed and guilt rob me of my happiness. I will not let unhappiness take command of my life. I will bounce back with FAITH and HOPE. I will TRIGGER HAPPINESS all the time, by doing things that will make me happy, as often as I can. I will SMILE and BE HAPPY today, and everyday of my Life!

Success through Sex Transmutation

Succcsex

by

RVM

How to use your own sex energy
to tap into the genius within!